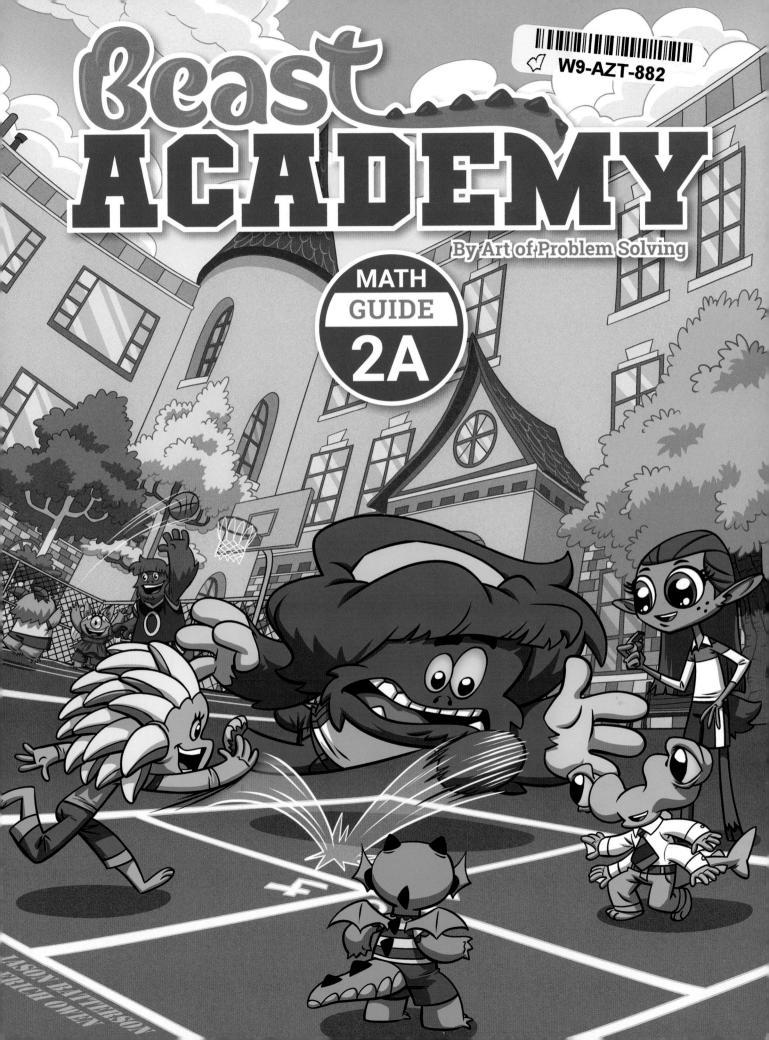

Published by: AoPS Incorporated
            10865 Rancho Bernardo Rd Ste 100
            San Diego, CA 92127-2102
            info@BeastAcademy.com

ISBN: 978-1-934124-30-7

Written by Jason Batterson
Illustrated by Erich Owen
Additional Illustrations by Paul Cox
Colored by Greta Selman

Visit the Beast Academy website at BeastAcademy.com.
Visit the Art of Problem Solving website at artofproblemsolving.com.
Printed in the United States of America.
2018 Printing.

Become a Math Beast!
For additional books,
printables, and more, visit
BeastAcademy.com

This is Guide 2A in a four-book series:

Guide 2A
Chapter 1: Place Value
Chapter 2: Comparing
Chapter 3: Addition

Guide 2B
Chapter 4: Subtraction
Chapter 5: Expressions
Chapter 6: Problem Solving

Guide 2C
Chapter 7: Measurement
Chapter 8: Strategies (+&−)
Chapter 9: Odds & Evens

Guide 2D
Chapter 10: Big Numbers
Chapter 11: Algorithms (+&−)
Chapter 12: Problem Solving

Now Available!
Beast Academy Online

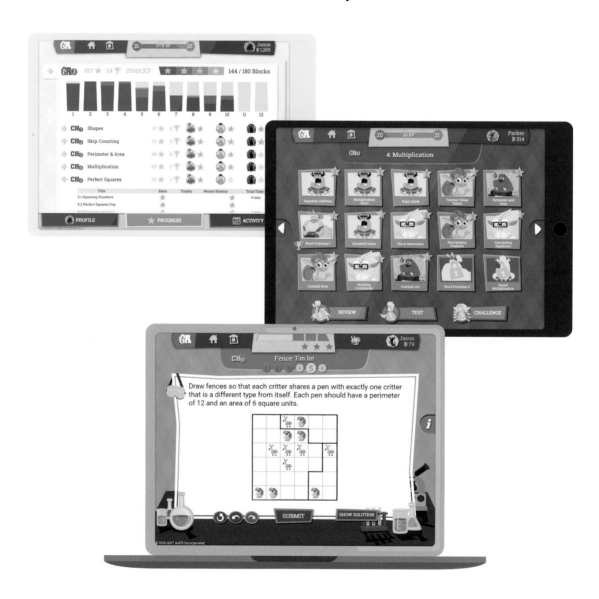

Learn more at BeastAcademy.com

Contents:

Characters 6

How to Use This Book 8

Chapter 1: Place Value 12

First Day 14

Pirate Numbers 16

Ones, Tens, Hundreds 24

Regrouping & Breaking 30

Chapter 2: Comparing 40

The Number Line 42

Distance Between 48

Iago 55

Comparing 56

Ordering 60

Chapter 3: Addition 68

Sums 70

Strategies 76

A Little Extra 82

Rearranging 88

Index 94

Alex
"The Executive"

IrOns his sOcks

Only wears
them tO bed

GrOgg (me!)

I can write with my feet! (nOt as well as with my hands)

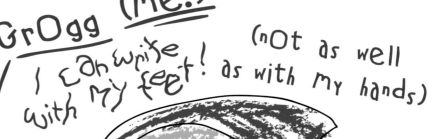

Winnie
"The Firecracker"

Testy at times

DOn't be fOOled
by her
cüte handwriting

Lizzie
"The BOOkwOrm"

Read all 52 bOOks
in the DragOn Diaries
series

wrOte new endings
fOr 3 Of them

Welcome to Beast Academy!

This book is called the Guide.

There is also a separate Practice book with lots of problems you can use to sharpen your skills.

The Guide is written like a comic book.

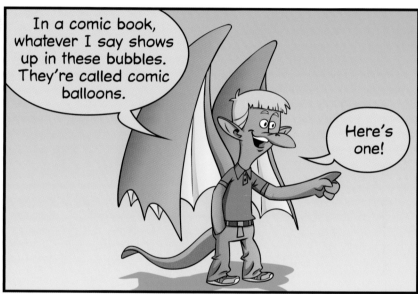

In a comic book, whatever I say shows up in these bubbles. They're called comic balloons.

Here's one!

Each character has a different balloon color. This makes it easy to tell who is talking.

My balloons are purple!

The story is told in panels.

Panels usually have a rectangular frame around them...

...like this one.

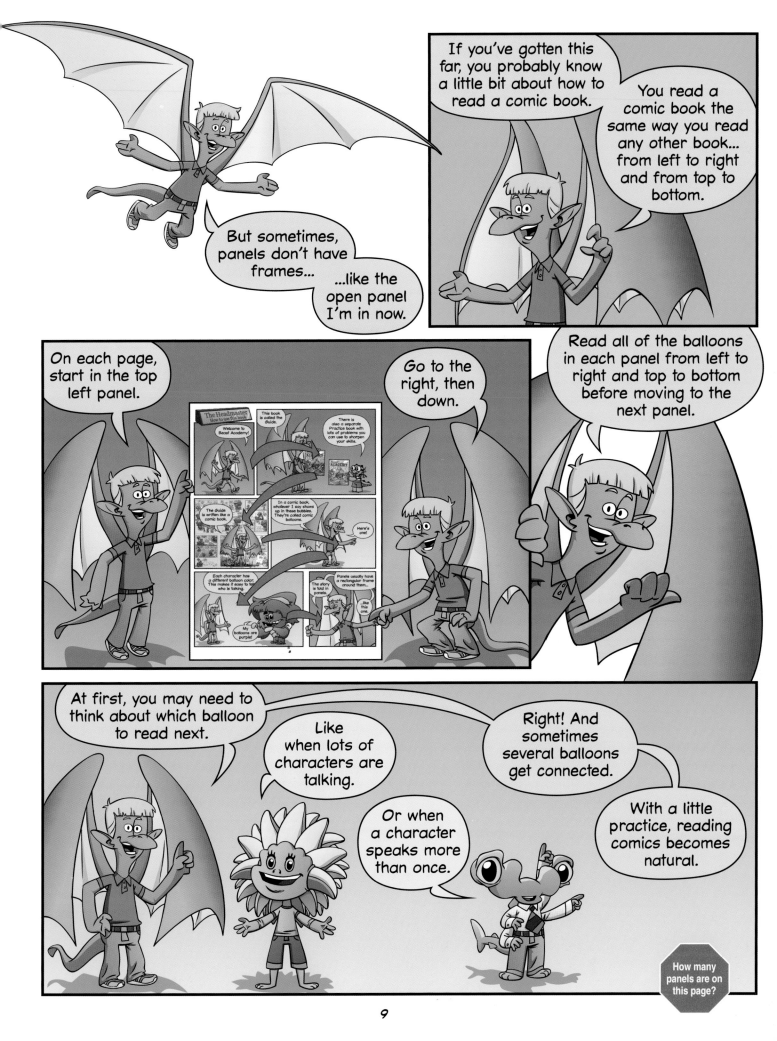

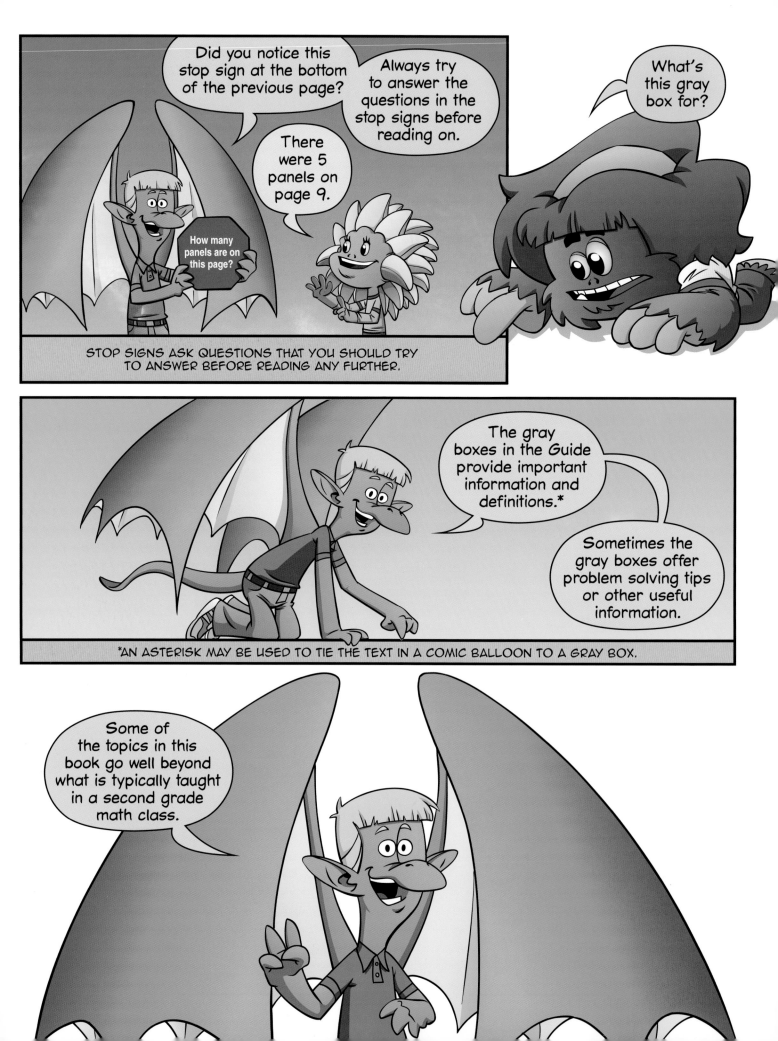

Contents: Chapter 1

See page 6 in the Practice book for a recommended
reading/practice sequence for Chapter 1.

First Day   14
What time is Woodshop class?

Pirate Numbers   16
How do you write fifty-six using pirate numbers?

Ones, Tens, Hundreds   24
What does the 3 in 37 stand for?

Regrouping & Breaking   30
Will subtracting ten from a number always
decrease its tens digit by one?

Chapter 1:
Place Value

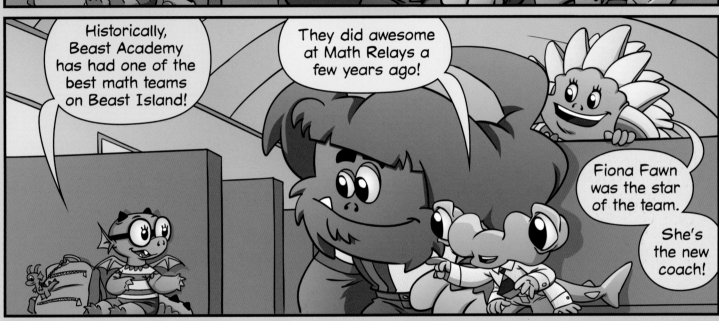

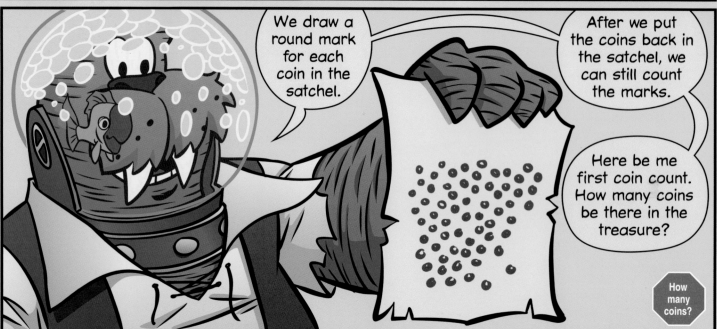

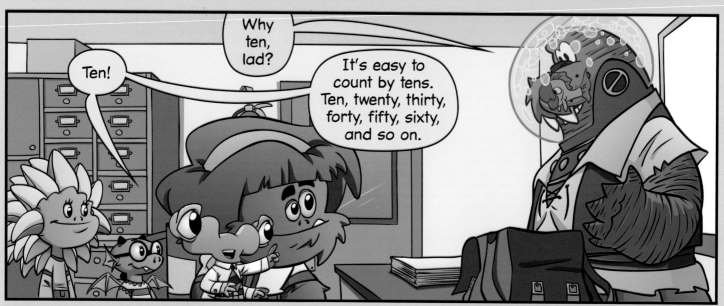

*COLUMNS GO UP AND DOWN ↕, AS SHOWN ABOVE. ROWS GO LEFT TO RIGHT ↔.

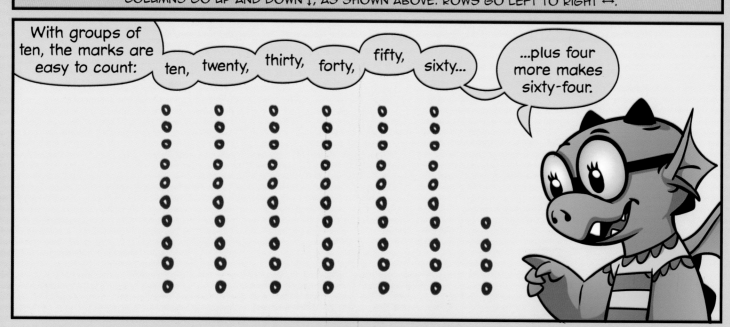

So, there were sixty-four coins in your first treasure.

Aye, well done.

Now, let's record the number o' coins in me most recent treasure.

I've given you each some coins. Record the number o' coins in your pile.

Done!

Already!?

Well... I didn't draw a mark for every single coin.

How will we be able to tell how many coins you counted?

19

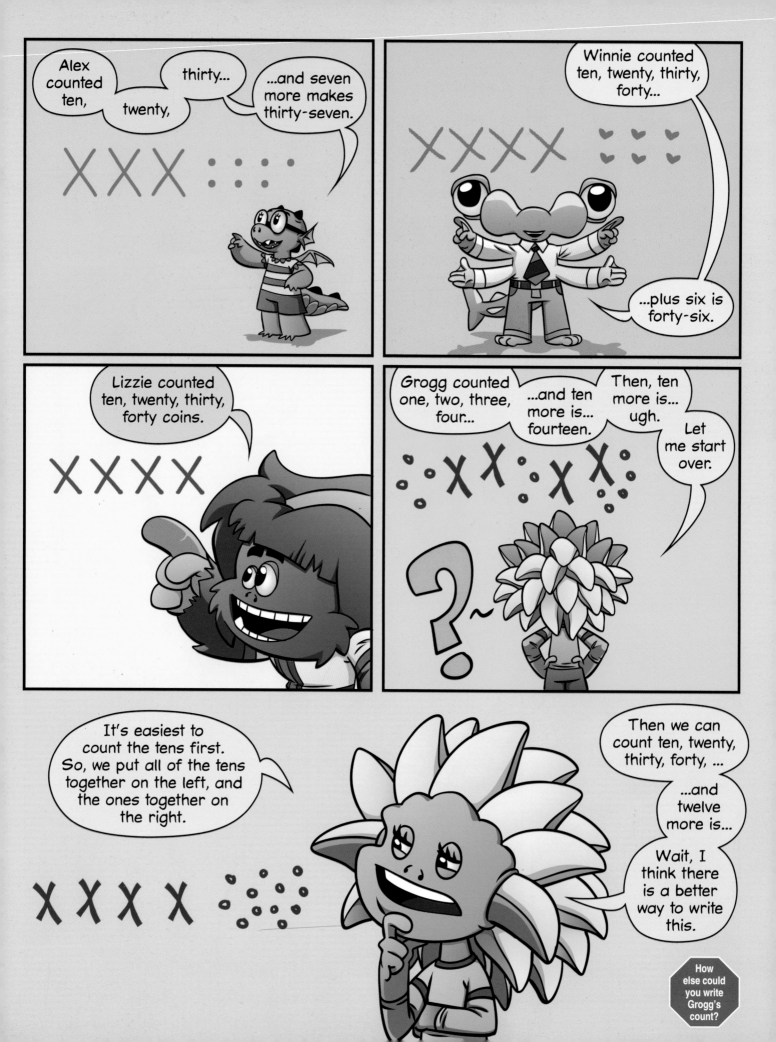

24

That's right. When most monsters talk about digits, they mean these ten symbols.

Digit:	Stands for:
0	zero
1	one
2	two
3	three
4	four
5	five
6	six
7	seven
8	eight
9	nine

That's a lot of symbols. Pirates only used three. Why do we need so many?

Using ten symbols, we can write even big numbers using only a few digits.

Let's look at Alex's coin count, for example. It takes three X's and seven dots to stand for thirty-seven coins.

Using digits, we can write a 3 and a 7 to mean the same thing.

That is a lot shorter.

What do the 3 and the 7 in 37 stand for?

Coins:
XXX ::::
37

What do the 3 and the 7 stand for?

That's right. In a three-digit number, the left digit tells you how many hundreds there are...

...the middle digit tells you how many tens there are...

...and the right digit tells you how many ones there are.

100 is the smallest three-digit number.

hundreds ↓ tens ↓ ones

100

There must be about 100 awards in this trophy case!

Whoa! Coach Fiona, is this you?

We're out of time! I'll see you all back here next week for practice.

29

Practice: Pages 12-17

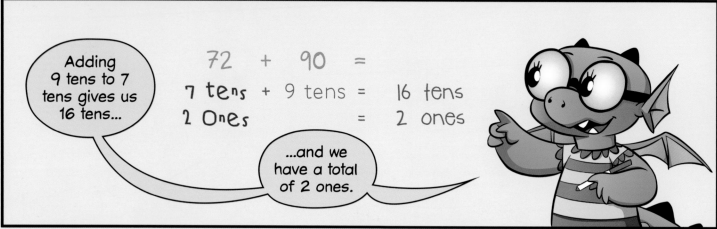

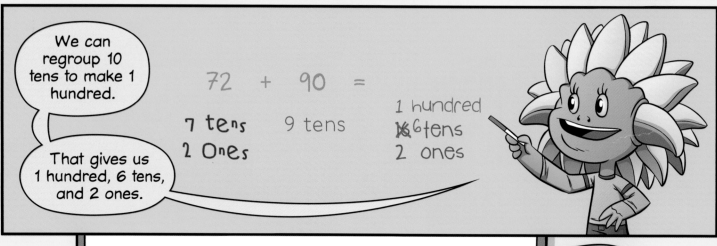

34

Excellent!

Next, let's try taking ten away.

47 magnets

There are forty-seven magnets on the whiteboard.

If we take ten away, how many magnets will be left on the board?

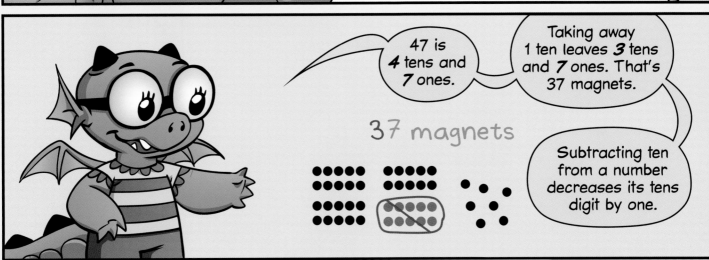

47 is **4** tens and **7** ones.

Taking away 1 ten leaves **3** tens and **7** ones. That's 37 magnets.

37 magnets

Subtracting ten from a number decreases its tens digit by one.

Very good. The symbol for subtraction is called a *minus sign*. 47 minus 10 looks like this.

When we subtract 10 from 47, the tens digit decreases by one and we get 37.

Will subtracting ten from a number *always* decrease its tens digit by one?

Not if the tens digit is a 0, like in 104.

Since there isn't a digit smaller than 0, we can't decrease the tens digit in 104.

How can we subtract 10 from 104?

$$47 - 10 = 37$$

$$104 - 10 =$$

Subtract 10 from 104.

35

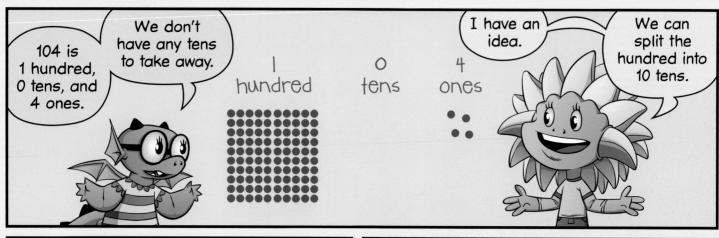

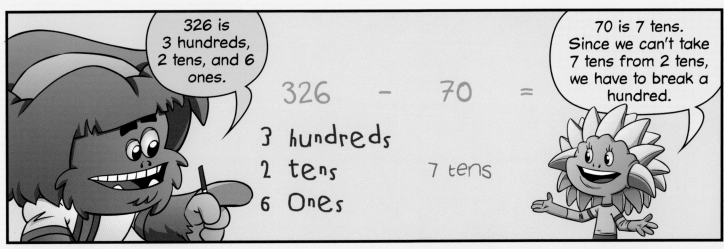

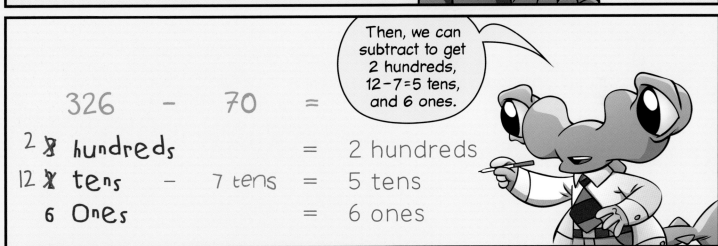

When we add numbers, sometimes we need to regroup 10 ones to make 1 ten...

58 + 7 = 65

5 tens
8 ones   7 ones   6 ~~5~~ tens
                            5 ~~15~~ ones

...or 10 tens to make 1 hundred.

62 + 70 = 132

6 tens   7 tens   1 hundred
2 ones   3 ~~13~~ tens
                            2 ones

And when we subtract numbers, sometimes we need to break 1 ten to make 10 ones...

64 - 7 = 57

5 ~~6~~ tens
14 ~~4~~ ones   7 ones   5 tens
                                   7 ones

...or 1 hundred to make 10 tens.

136 - 50 = 86

0 ~~1~~ hundred
13 ~~3~~ tens   5 tens   8 tens
6 ones   6 ones

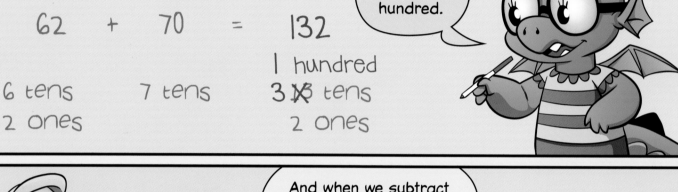

Contents: Chapter 2

See page 36 in the Practice book for a recommended reading/practice sequence for Chapter 2.

The Number Line   42
What whole number is to the left of 25 on the number line?

Distance Between   48
What number is halfway between 54 and 98?

Iago   55
You have a penny on 21. Where can you place a second penny to capture the dime on 25?

Comparing   56
What symbols are used to compare numbers that are not equal?

Ordering   60
After 888 and 889, what is the third-smallest three-digit number that uses only 8's and 9's?

Chapter 2:
Comparing

WHOLE NUMBERS START AT 0 AND GO ON FOREVER: 0, 1, 2, 3, 4, 5, ...AND SO ON.

We can use this rod to measure the distance between **consecutive numbers**.

I see. We can start by drawing a mark for 0. Then, the length of this rod is the distance to the next mark.

CONSECUTIVE NUMBERS COME ONE AFTER ANOTHER. FOR EXAMPLE, 23 AND 24 ARE CONSECUTIVE.

Yep.

Uh oh. I lost track. What mark are we on?

I'm not sure.

I have an idea that will make it easier for us to keep track.

If we make every tenth mark longer than the others...

...it will be easier to know how many we've drawn.

I see. The long marks start at 0 and mark the tens...

0...

...10...

...20...

...30...

...40...

...so, we're at 44.

Let's finish up.

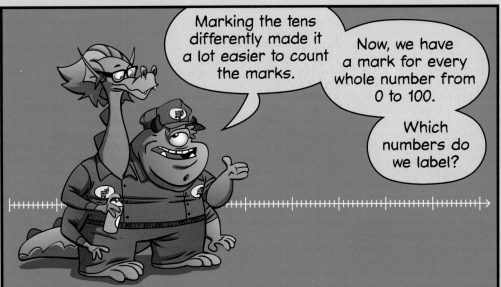

49

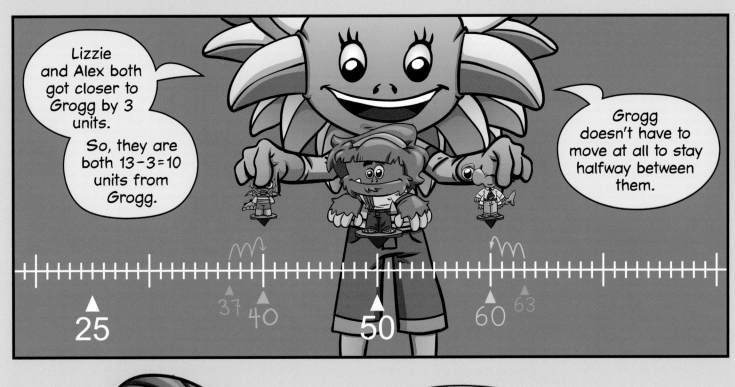

Lizzie and Alex both got closer to Grogg by 3 units.

So, they are both 13−3=10 units from Grogg.

Grogg doesn't have to move at all to stay halfway between them.

Good. When Lizzie and Alex move toward each other by the same amount, the number that is halfway between them doesn't change.

We can use this to help us find the number that is halfway between two numbers.

For example, if Lizzie stands at 56, and Alex stands at 94, what number is halfway between them?

Try it.

52

We can count up from 54 and down from 98 to find the middle.

The number that is halfway between 54 and 98...

...is the same as the number that is halfway between 64 and 88...

...or 74 and 78...

...which is 76!

10 10 2 2 10 10

54 64 74 76 78 88 98

Great! We can use number line strategies without an actual number line.

For example, how could you figure out whether 44 is closer to 10 or to 80?

We can see if 44 is smaller or larger than the number that is halfway between 10 and 80.

The number that is halfway between 10 and 80 is also halfway between 20 and 70...

...and 30 and 60...

...and 40 and 50...

...which is 45.

44 is less than 45, so 44 is closer to 10 than to 80.

10 10 10 5 5 10 10 10

10 20 30 40 45 50 60 70 80

↑
44

I did something different.

I started at 44 and counted *out* towards 10 and 80.

Practice: Pages 37-49

RECESS

In the game of Iago, two players take turns placing coins on a number line and capturing their opponent's coins. The player with the most coins on the number line when the line is full wins.

Setup

The game is played on a number line with ten numbered marks. Each player begins with a set of game pieces. For example, Player 1 can use pennies, and Player 2 can use dimes.

Play

Players take turns placing one of their own coins on the number line until the number line is full.

Players can capture each other's coins. To capture a dime, Player 1 must place a penny so that a dime is halfway between the new penny and a penny that was already on the number line. To capture a penny, Player 2 must place a dime so that a penny is halfway between the new dime and a dime that was already on the number line.

For example, it is Player 2's turn to place a dime on the board below:

By placing a dime on 23, Player 2 can capture the penny on 25 and replace it with a dime.

— or —

By placing a dime on 29, Player 2 can capture the pennies on 25 and 28! Both are replaced with dimes.

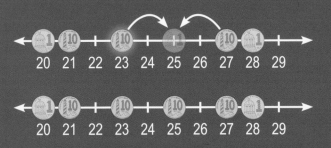

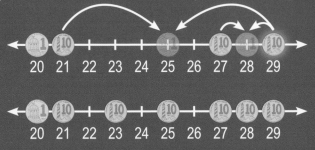

When a coin is replaced, the new coin is not used to create extra captures on the same turn.

Winning

Play continues until there is one coin on each number. The player with the most coins on the number line wins. If players have the same number of coins, the game ends in a tie. *Print game boards and find variations at BeastAcademy.com.*

THE < SYMBOL MEANS "IS LESS THAN" AND THE > SYMBOL MEANS "IS GREATER THAN."

Very good. We use the greater than and less than symbols to compare two amounts that are not equal.

As Lizzie said, the arrow always points to the smaller number.

$$5 < 6$$
$$65 > 56$$
$$6+5 < 65$$

Can anyone think of another good way to remember which way the symbol goes?

The symbol has a small side and a big side.

The smaller number always goes on the small side, and the bigger number goes on the big side.

The less than symbol looks kind of like a crooked "L" for "less."

I think the symbol looks like a big mouth that wants to eat the bigger number.

CHOMP!

Those are great ways to remember!

Which symbol belongs in each circle below?

100 ◯ 200

12+23 ◯ 34

543 ◯ 534+10

Try all three.

58

When we compare numbers, the bigger place values matter more than the smaller ones.

For example, 54 and 45 have the same digits.

But, since 54 has more tens, 54 is bigger.

$$54 > 45$$

Any number in the 50's is bigger than any number in the 40's.

And for three-digit numbers, the number with more hundreds is always bigger.

Any number in the 300's or 400's is bigger than 299.

So, 299 is the third-smallest number.

In order, the three smallest numbers are 45, 54, and 299.

(299)   (54)   333

344   452   (45)

341   352   325

Aye. We compare numbers usin' the digits in each place value, startin' with the largest place value.

Now, which be the three **biggest** numbers?

Maybe we should write the numbers with their digits lined up.

299   54   333

344   452   45

341   352   325

Find the three largest numbers.

It's easier to compare the numbers when we line them up, like this.

299
54
333
344
452
45
341
352
325

Great idea! Then, it's easy to compare the digits in each place value.

Exactly! To order the numbers, we start by looking at their hundreds digits.

Two numbers are less than 100.

Only one number is in the 200's.

There are five numbers in the 300's.

And there's only one number in the 400's.

Can you put all nine numbers in order?

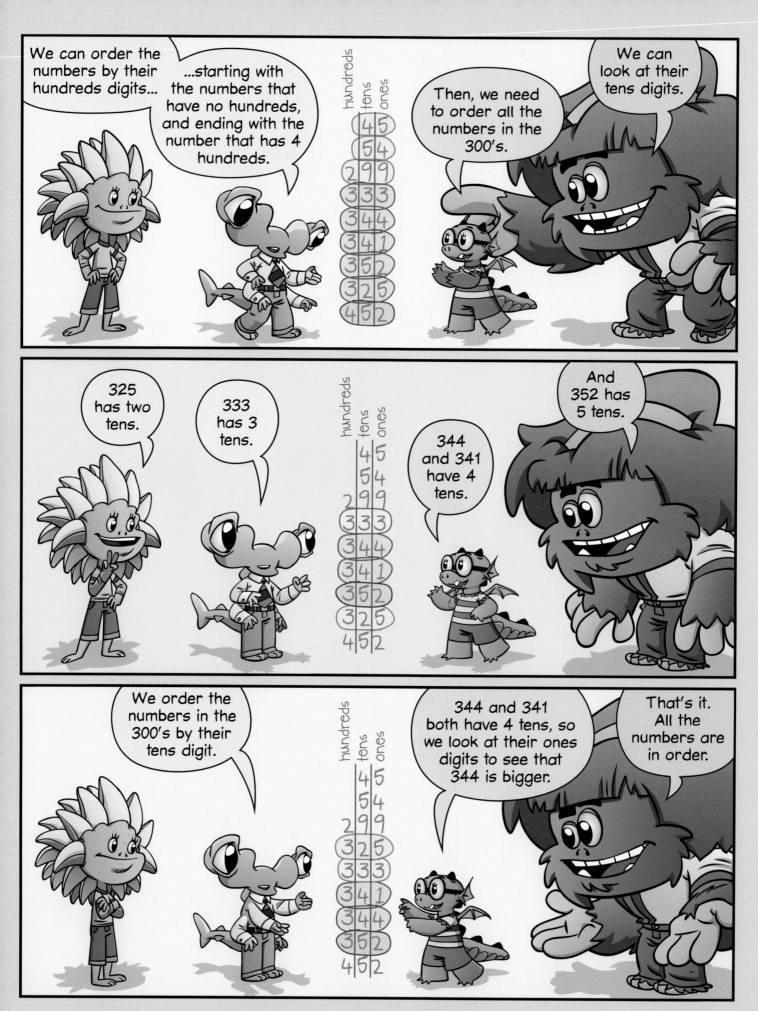

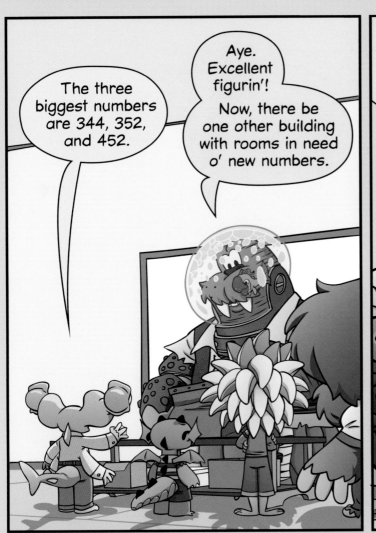

The three biggest numbers are 344, 352, and 452.

Aye. Excellent figurin'! Now, there be one other building with rooms in need o' new numbers.

The labs in the science building all need new numbers. Each room be havin' a different three-digit number.

The lab numbers use only the digits 8 'n' 9. How many three-digit numbers use only the digits 8 'n' 9?

Let's see, there's 888, and 999...

...and 989, and 898...

...and 888...

You already said that one.

We should organize our work to make sure we don't miss any. Let's try listing all of the numbers in order.

List in order all of the 3-digit numbers that use only the digits 8 and 9.

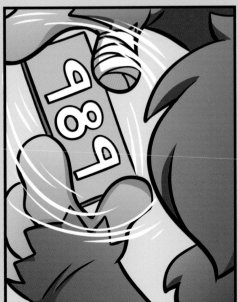

Practice: Pages 50-63

Contents: Chapter 3

See page 64 in the Practice book for a recommended reading/practice sequence for Chapter 3.

Sums   70
What number has 7 tens and 13 ones?

Strategies   76
What easier addition problem can we use to help us add 75+128?

A Little Extra   82
The sum of 298+498 is four less than what number?

Rearranging   88
Can you find an easy way to add 14+14+16+16?

PIRATE LEAGUE

SUMS

One coin.

X Ten coins.

C One Hundred coins.

Weeks ago, you helped me count coins usin' pirate symbols.

Today, we'll learn how to find a sum.

Some what?

A **sum**.

Huh?

A **sum** is the result you get when you add two or more numbers.

Rankings

1,338

Marauder *1,215*

...lin' Bonnie

Tusky McTusks

Jolly Joe

Aye. A sum be the result of addition.
Here be the coin counts you made.
Let's begin by findin' the sum o' Winnie's coins 'n' Lizzie's coins.

Coins:
XXXX ♥♥♥
=46

Coins:
XXX ::::
=37

Coins:
XXXX
=40

Coins:
XXXXX°°
=52

Try it.

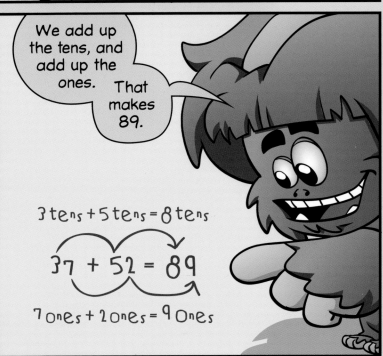

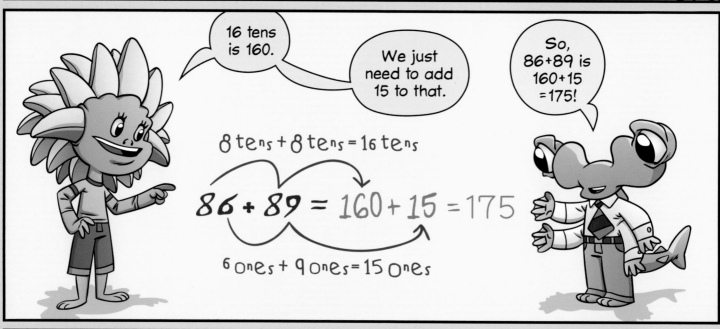

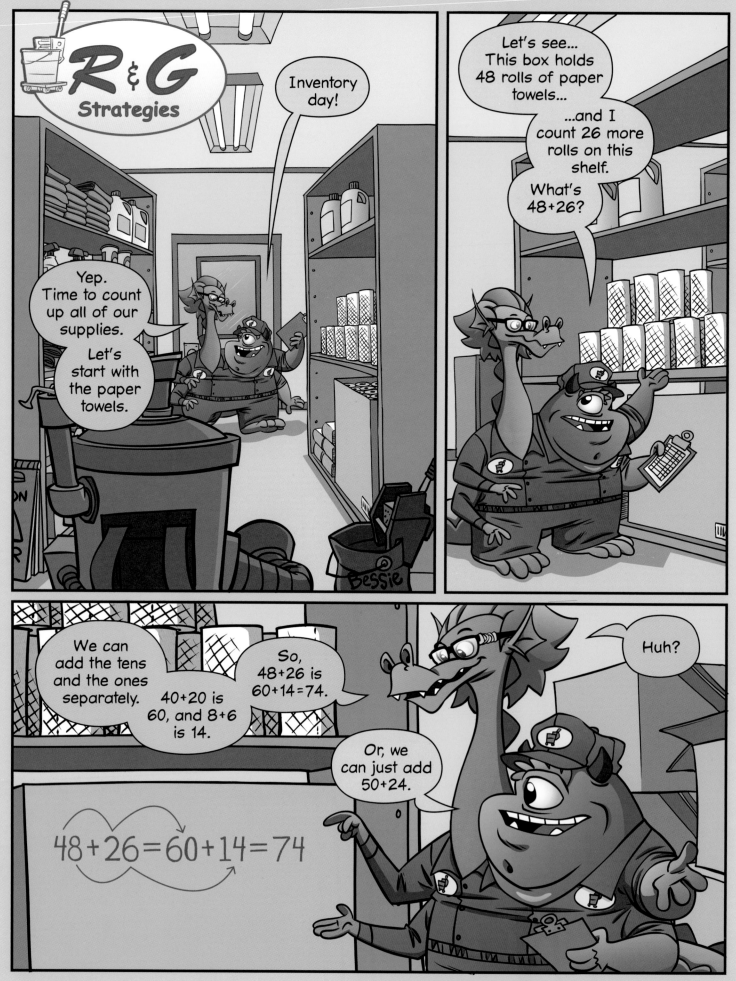

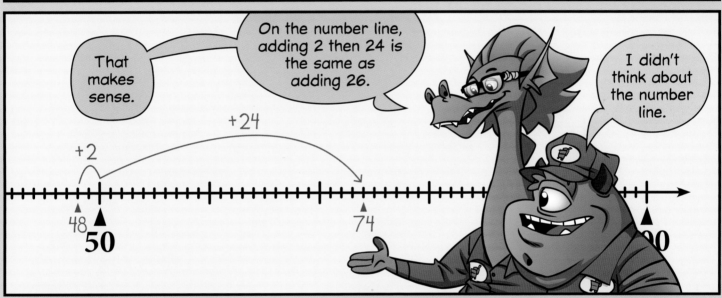

That's a nice trick! Let's see if it helps us count some more items.

Are we low on rubber gloves?

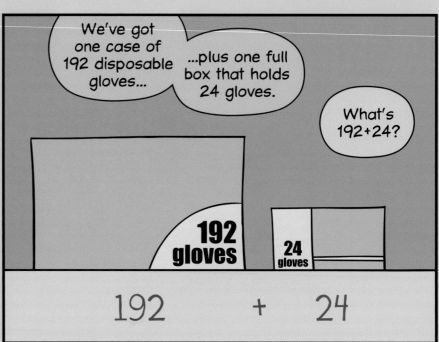

We've got one case of 192 disposable gloves...

...plus one full box that holds 24 gloves.

What's 192+24?

192 + 24

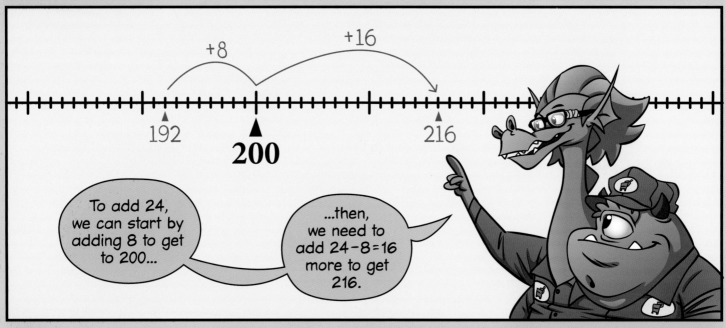

+8

+16

192

200

216

To add 24, we can start by adding 8 to get to 200...

...then, we need to add 24−8=16 more to get 216.

Or, to make the addition easier, we can just take 8 gloves from the box...

192 + 24

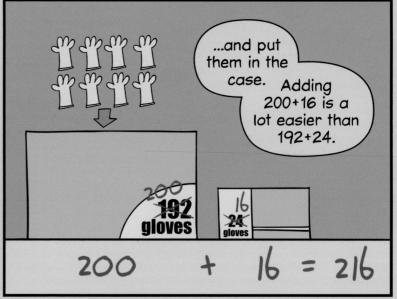

...and put them in the case. Adding 200+16 is a lot easier than 192+24.

200 + 16 = 216

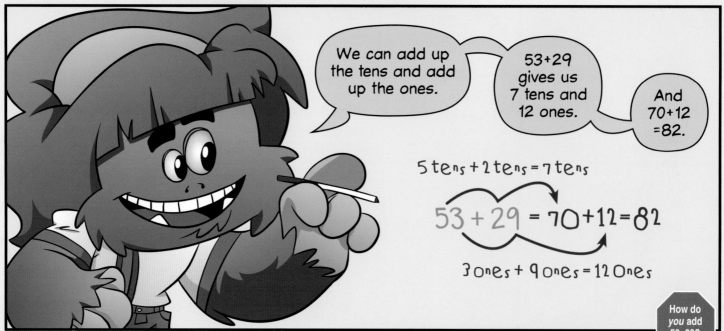

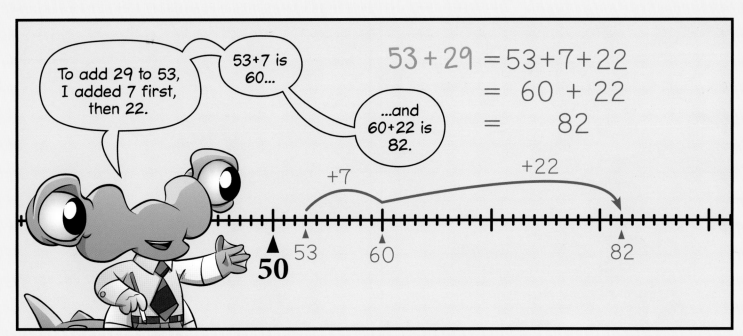

Adding 30 is a lot easier than adding 29.

And adding 29 is the same as adding 30, then taking 1 away.

$$53 + 29 = 53 + 30 - 1$$
$$= 83 - 1$$
$$= 82$$

So, to add 53+29, we can start by adding 53+30 to get 83.

Then, we subtract 1 to get 82.

Excellent! Many addition problems are easier if you add a little extra...

...then take it away.

362+9
233+90
575+97
298+498

How could you use this strategy to find each of these sums?

Try all four.

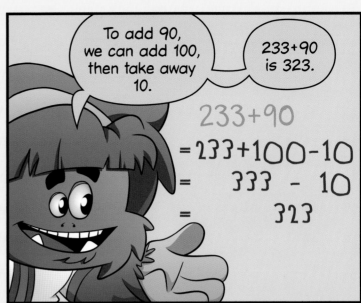

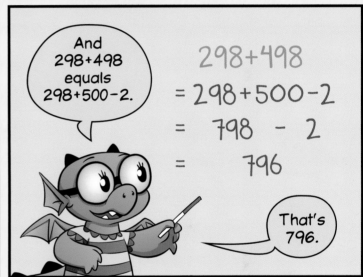

$$50+50+50+50+50+50=300$$

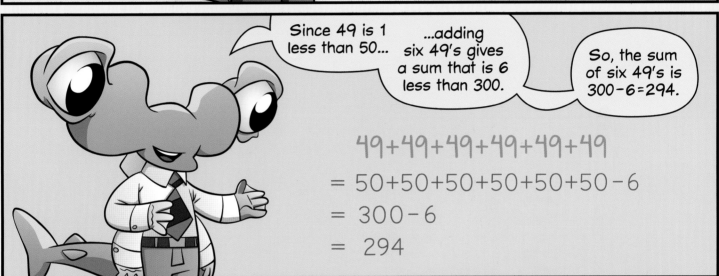

$$49+49+49+49+49+49$$
$$= 50+50+50+50+50+50-6$$
$$= 300-6$$
$$= 294$$

Practice: Pages 70-85

*MATH BEASTS CALL THIS THE *COMMUTATIVE PROPERTY OF ADDITION*.
YOU DON'T NEED TO REMEMBER WHAT IT'S CALLED TO KNOW THAT IT WORKS.

*THIS IS CALLED THE **ASSOCIATIVE PROPERTY OF ADDITION**. TOGETHER, THE COMMUTATIVE AND ASSOCIATIVE PROPERTIES OF ADDITION LET US ADD NUMBERS IN ANY ORDER WE WANT.

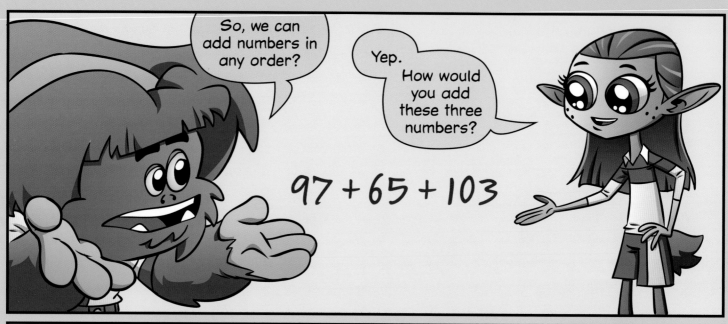

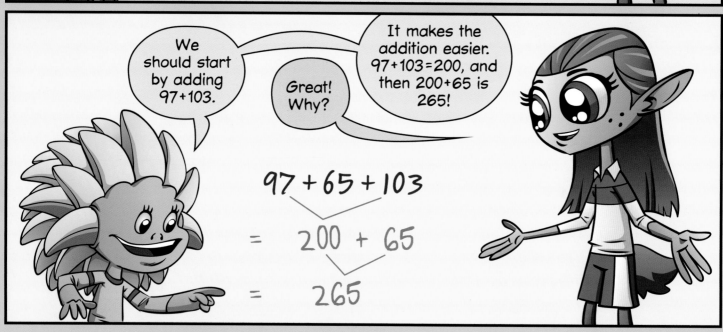

19 + 17 + 3
= 19 + 20
= 39

35 + 26 + 35
= 70 + 26
= 96

14 + 14 + 16 + 16
= 30 + 30
= 60

11 + 4 + 11 + 6 + 11
= 33 + 10
= 43

$6 + 7 + 8 + 9 + 10 + 11 + 12 + 13 + 14$

$99 + 10 + 99 + 20 + 99 + 30 + 99 + 40$

$6+7+8+9+10+11+12+13+14$

$= 20$

For this one, we can pair 6 with 14 to make 20.

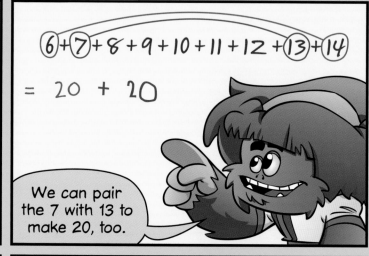

$6+7+8+9+10+11+12+13+14$

$= 20 + 20$

We can pair the 7 with 13 to make 20, too.

$6+7+8+9+10+11+12+13+14$

$= 20 + 20 + 20$

8+12 is 20.

$6+7+8+9+10+11+12+13+14$

$= 20 + 20 + 20 + 20 + 10$

So is 9+11.

The only number without a partner is 10.

So, we get 20+20+20+20+10 =90.

$6+7+8+9+10+11+12+13+14$

$= 20 + 20 + 20 + 20 + 10$

$= 90$

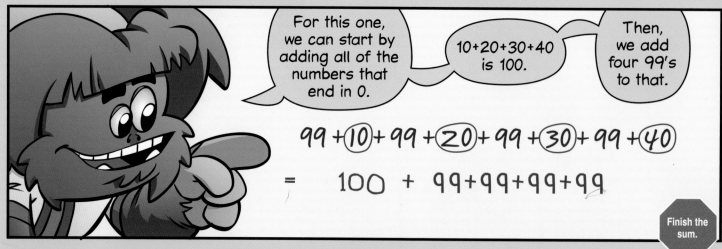

For this one, we can start by adding all of the numbers that end in 0.

10+20+30+40 is 100.

Then, we add four 99's to that.

$99 + 10 + 99 + 20 + 99 + 30 + 99 + 40$

$= 100 + 99 + 99 + 99 + 99$

Finish the sum.

Index

Symbols

–, 35
+, 31
<, 57–59
=, 56
>, 57–59

A

addition
 adding 1 ten, 30–32
 adding more than 1 ten, 33–34
 associative property, 89
 by place value, 70–76, 82
 commutative property, 88
 on the number line, 77–78, 83
 regrouping, 32–34, 38, 73
 strategies, 76–80, 82–87, 88–93
 with subtraction, 84–87
associative property of addition, 89

B

Beast Academy Online, 4
bicycles, 39
breaking (in subtraction), 36–38

C

candles, 39
cannonball!, 81
Captain Kraken. See Woodshop
columns, 18
commutative property of addition,
 88
comparing numbers, 56–59
consecutive, 44
counting
 by tens, 18, 22–23, 44, 46
 up, down, in, and out, 53
C (pirate symbol), 23, 70

D

digits, 24–29, 61–64
distance
 halfway between, 50–54
 on the number line, 49–54
dot (pirate symbol), 20

E

electricity, 39
equals sign, 56
eyebrows, 39

F

Fiona. See Math Team
fizzing mop bucket tablets, 79–81
food drive, 82

G

greater than (>), 57–59

H

halfway between, 50–54, 55
Headmaster, 8–11
hundreds, 28–29

I

Iago, 55
index, 94–95

K

Kraken. See Woodshop

L

less than (<), 57–59

M

magical items, 30, 39
magicians, 39
magnets, 30–39
marshmallows, 39
math bots, 93
Math Team
 Distance Between, 48–54
 Ones, Tens, Hundreds, 24–29
 Rearranging, 88–93
minus sign, 35
Ms. Q.
 A Little Extra, 82–87
 Comparing, 56–59
 Regrouping & Breaking, 30–39

N

number line, 42–47, 48–55
>addition, 77–78, 83
>distance, 49–54
>marks, 43–45
>unit, 50

Number Line Dodgeball Tag, 41, 54
numbers
>comparing, 56–59
>consecutive, 44
>digits, 24–29, 61–64
>number line, 42–47, 48–55
>ordering, 60–67
>pirate, 16–23
>place value, 27–29
>whole, 42

O

ordering
>addition, 88–93
>numbers, 60–67

P

Pirate League, 69, 75
pirate numbers, 16–23
place value, 27–29
plus sign, 31

R

rearranging addition, 88–93
Recess
>Iago, 55
regrouping, 32–34, 38, 73
R&G
>Strategies, 76–81
>The Number Line, 42–47
rows, 18

S

School Bus
>First Day, 14–15
soap bubbles, 39
subtraction
>breaking, 36–38
>taking away 1 ten, 35–36
>taking away more than 1 ten, 36–38
>with addition, 84–87

sum, 70–75, 76–80, 84–87, 90–92
symbols
>=, <, and >, 56–59
>digits, 24–29
>pirate numbers, 16–23, 70–73

T

take away. See subtraction
thermoses, 39
trophy case, 29

U

Uncle Herman, 39
units, 50

W

whole numbers, 42
Woodshop
>Ordering, 60–67
>Pirate Numbers, 16–23
>Sums, 70–75

X

X (pirate symbol), 20–27, 70–73

For additional books,
printables, and more, visit
BeastAcademy.com